Home Without A Home

by

Tim Connelly

ISBN 978-1-4357-3130-1

Bill

I am a veteran of the Vietnam war.
I was in detox last month, then in a halfway house.
I use to wake up drinking and went to bed drinking.
My energy was slowly leaving my body.
I had just enough strength to get out of bed and grab a beer.
You know one in four homeless Americans are veterans.
More veterans are coming home from war
and things are not likely to get any better.
We have not learned our lesson from Vietnam
and the same thing is happening all over again.

Denny

I have diabetes and skin cancer.
I never associated it with Agent Orange.
My son has spina bifida.
I'm 58 years old and have had four heart attacks.
I'm not bitter.
My war wounds came from my government.
I was a 19 year old Army engineer in Vietnam.
A lot of friends have died from cancer from other there.
I lost my job two years ago.
Then fought a battle with the bureaucracy for benefits.
I will probably be dead in ten years.
I enjoy myself and live for today and not tomorrow.

Mike

I suffer from lung cancer.
I’m disabled but alive.
It’s nothing I can’t live with.
Vietnam veterans are overwhelming veteran centers.
Terrorist attacks of 9/11 and the war in Iraq are the triggers
It’s never to late but sooner the better though.
Aging has become a factor.
We are in our late 50’s.
Our needs have drastically changed.
I was in the Coast Guard in Vietnam.
I started to cough three years ago and spit up blood.
I’ve undergone radiation therapy
and two thirds of my lung is gone.
It’s been a horrible experience.
I will be short of breath the rest of my days on earth
but its better than no breath at all.
I can’t give up on life

Mark

So many men who have suffered for years in silence.
They don't know why they suffer daily.
It always affects their home life and jobs.
I live in a new home for veterans.
A place to form a family and start over.
It's a colonial-style house
near a doctor's office and residence.
A home for four.
I am the only resident.
I work part-time and am a disabled Vietnam veteran
who's clean and sober. I get 800 dollars a month.
Where are you going to live on that?
I want to rebuild family values
and look at how I got to be where I am.
But there's no one to pamper me.
It's a last step in getting out
of the being homeless process
and back to the mainstream.

Lynn

My mission is to help homeless veterans.
A childhood friend had nowhere to sleep.
My friend John struggled on the streets.
It will never happen to me I thought.
I couldn't believe a friend I grew up with was homeless.
When you see things like that it brings out what you want to do.
My fund-raising has been meager but I have hopes to build a shelter.
A million dollar goal.
I want this to be a beginning.
200,000 veterans homeless in this country.
Affordable housing is a problem.
Many veterans suffer mental distress
and disconnect from family and friends
which adds to the likelihood of homelessness.
They go and serve then when they come home,
they've changed. I remain optimistic.
The key to success is to make people realize
veterans were willing to sacrifice their lives.
It's unfair to leave them out on the streets.
A community owes veterans more than memorials on holidays.
I don't want America to remember them,
I want America to help them.

Gary and William

A few days ago
he found his homeless friend
dead at the shopping plaza.
Today,
the 55 year old homeless veteran
was found dead himself
in the same plaza.
Gary found William, his friend, dead
behind a pet store.
Gary was found dead
near a supermarket on the plaza.
His last known address
was the Veterans Hospital
Officials say Gary died of natural causes.
His friend died of heart disease.

John

I once dodged bullets for this country in Vietnam.
I dodge cockroaches in a flea-bag motel now days.
I am stuck in Room 103.
I can't find a place to stay in the city.
I'm homeless. I'm homeless.
Stuck in a rat-infested place.
I'm like hundreds of veterans in the City
living in cars, motels or on the street.
I know one veteran who lives at a dorm
for employees of the race track.
Another veteran wanders down Broadway.
I know of some veterans who camp in the woods.
Vets are living with their brothers and sisters
because they can't afford rent.
They are too proud to say they are hurting.
People are at their ropes end
for a warm place with food.
We do the best we can says family services.
I have practically given up.
I just have a cardboard box of possessions
in my motel room.
I'm troubled by the stress of a long lost war.
I take a van to the VA hospital and look for an apartment.
I try not to come back to Room 103
until the traffic and shouting coming through the paper-thin walls
quiets at night.

Marty

The closest thing I have to an address
is my mail box inside the Mail Box store on Chicago Avenue.
I am 59 years old and I am a Vietnam veteran
and retired government employee.
I resent being called an eyesore.
My wife is blind.
We have been homeless since November
and live in the Regional Park.
It's a traumatic experience.
I thought I was going to die several times
after some recent severe storms.
The wind was blowing hard
and we were protected only with a drop cloth.
I don't know where me and my wife will go tomorrow
when the park is closed for clean up work.
I have no place to stay.
I can't drive. I have no bus pass.
We are treated like dirt
because we have no control of our lives.
We can't help the way we are.
We are human beings.
I've tried everything.
It's rich against poor.
I served my country in Vietnam.
I got decorated.
No one cares that I am a veteran or disabled or old.
I am treated like a criminal.
We go to the park each night
and leave at dawn pushing a cart with our belongings
to the shopping center to our mailbox
hoping to find something in the mail
like a little bit of money.

Paul

The newspaper headline declares
our county has eight thousand millionaires.
It's one of the wealthiest in the country,
no wonder it's front page news.
Some news doesn't make the headlines.
About 400 people in the county
spent last night in the woods.
They have no homes.
Most have jobs.
The jobs are marginal.
They do not pay much and do not last long hours.
It's a hard life.
I am a Marine Corps veteran.
I have lived in hotel rooms, friends houses
and in the woods. I have worked
as a carpenter and mover.
Recently I worked on a masonry crew
until a car knocked me off my bike
and I broke some ribs.
I'm waiting for a trip to the veterans hospital.
If I can get an appointment
or if I can schedule a seat on the county bus
and if I can make it four miles to the Service Center
at 7:00 a.m. to catch the bus.

Dave and Bill

A pickup truck struck and killed two homeless men
outside a downtown homeless center.
The driver was guilty of capital murder
for the deaths of Dave and Bill
because he had been chasing another man
when the truck veered onto a sidewalk
and struck the two men.
These people in our society are invisible.
We don't see them in our everyday lives.
These people are living, breathing human beings
with the right to live in our society.
For whatever reason they were out on the street.
With the truck racing behind him,
a fleeing man jumped up on a stretch of sidewalk
where the homeless gather and sleep.
The truck struck the two homeless men
and crashed into the homeless center.
Dave was dead immediately,
while Bill died from injuries the next day.
Both of the men were military veterans
who had become homeless late in their lives
after suffering minor strokes.
When not staying with friends or relatives,
their home was a stretch of sidewalk
outside the homeless center.
Dave was just a week from moving off the streets
into an apartment when he was killed.
Those who knew the men described then
as generous far beyond their means.
They were not nameless nothings on the street.
They were not criminals.
They raised children.
They had a life.

Dennis

Tanks is dangerous.
Everything inside moves. Everything.
I would use alcohol to bury the memories.
I thought I had a pretty good handle on things.
I thought.
I don't blame the Army for my alcoholism.
The Army exposed me to things I didn't expect
and left me to cope with them on my own.
It's taken years for me to figure out what exactly changed me.
During that time I lost my sobriety, my family and my home.
They say you see death and it traumatizes some people.
My problem was that I would bury what I had done
and what I had seen happen.
I saw men get messed up and sent home
with no legs torn up by tanks.
There was always death in this crap.
I was taught that you keep your feelings buried.
You don't tell nobody nothing.
You don't trust nobody.
I didn't know no better.
I thought God, country, drinking raising hell
-- that was just all part of life.
Little did I know how things were going to take a drastic change.
I hadn't experienced anything that had to do with death.
It did bother me as time passed.
I hit the road after the Army.
Done lost my license.
Done lost my life.
Done lost my wife.
Done lost my kids.
Done lost my whole family.
I went from state to state
living in motels and getting drunk.
I passed out on the sides of roads and in ditches.
I got use to having nothing
not so much as a pencil, a comb, a knife

or a dime to my name.
One night in a homeless shelter
I thought You know, I really ain't gittin' nowhere
and I don't want to go back home.
There was nothing left there for me.
I was sick and tired of living with people,
traveling across the states.
I was sick and tired of people not understanding me.
They didn't know who I was.
They hadn't seen what I had done.
They hadn't looked at where I had been.
I have been sober 17 months.

Tom

I live in transitional housing.
It took time to get addicted and drop into despair.
It takes time to get out.
I joined the Army in 1975
after I dropped out of high school
and could only find minimum wage work.
I think spirituality is the first thing
to go out the door with addiction
and the last thing to come back.
You drink. You drug. You feel guilty.
You drink more. You stop talking to God
because you feel why would he talk to me
I'm not doing anything right.
You have got to give in to win, man.
Pride can't stop you from getting help.
If the alcohol doesn't get you physically
it gets you mentally.
If it doesn't get you mentally,
it just keeps moving through you.
The best way to defeat your enemy
is to know your enemy.
I help transport infirm veterans
to their doctor appointment.
It's the only job I have ever loved.
Helping other veterans for some reason helps me.
I'm hopeful, even happy for the first time
in a long time. Guys lose their kids, their wives,
the people they love but there comes a time,
though, when it is possible
to imagine those kinds of love returning.
My family feels better because I feel better.
It's wonderful the way one thing can trickle on another.
I may be the little pebble that drops in the water
but the rings get larger each day
I am clean and sober.

The Brotherhood

Homeless veterans of the war in Iraq
are showing up in homeless shelters
around the country.
There is fear they are the leading edge
of a new generation of homeless veterans
not seen since Vietnam.
It is happening and this nation is not prepared.
It is only the crest of the wave.
It is what happened with Vietnam veterans.
John went to Vietnam.
It's like watching history being repeated.
Luis has lived out of his truck on and off
for three months since returning from Iraq.
One day he had a home and the next day
he was on the streets.
Shrapnel nearly severed his left thumb
and he still has trouble moving it
and shrapnel still comes out once in a while.
Luis felt pushed out of the military.
He didn't get the medical care he needed for his hand
and he would later learn his mind.
They treated them like cattle a rush,
it was all about numbers instead of quality care.
They said let the VA take care of it.
He went to the VA and it was full.
They would call him.
James fought with the Marines in Iraq and Afghanistan.
Mental stress is the hardest part.
Civilians died, men women and kid.
It's something hard to live with.

Bob

I left for war in 1966 a boy
and came back a drunkard,
pill-popper and cocaine addict.
My former boss and former wife
will tell you I came back
an all-around pain in the ass
with a vicious temper
and venomous mouth
I couldn't control.
My mother took me in
when I couldn't afford a place
to live because paying for booze
and dope came first.
I might have ended up homeless
That's what war does to you.
That's what combat can do.
Behind a haunting blue-eyed stare,
he offered his warning to soldiers fighting
America's new war on terror
and those who will go later.

Rick

I was shivering with addictions
and left behind all of my possessions
at a motel along the Lake Road
last winter and walked 20 miles
in the snow.
I felt I would soon be dead.
I had no illusions about it.
I'm an Army veteran
a heroin and crack addict.
I called my brother a half dozen times
pleading for help.
My brother finally drove me to the VA.
The military got me into this mess
maybe it could help me out of it.
Did I have hope?
I stared at the floor for several minutes
and found an answer.
I served in Germany in the 1970s
where I learned to drink and left the service
with little direction beyond consuming drugs.
It's been ten months,
I work and have reconnected
with my family.
I garden and do photography
and help prepare food at the homeless shelter.
I knew 40 veterans who were in my situation
who have died.
I feel fortunate to be here.

Thomas

I wonder if there can ever be an end to homelessness.
I am doubtful. It is a never ending problem.
It isn't something that can be solved in ten years...
the afflicted, the poor and the needy
will be with us always.
The costs of war are not helping.
The government should take care of its own people.
War hasn't solved any problems that I know of.
There are bad wars, but there are no bad veterans.
The country ought to protect the person who served.

Gary

I served eight years in the military
and am extremely proud of my service.
The work ethic and camaraderie can't be replaced.
A lot of people come together
and I miss that.
Still, I left the military
with drug and alcohol addictions.
My turning point came in Kansas
while living with my alcoholic uncle.
My uncle pleaded with me
not to end up like him.
Shortly after, I sought treatment.
I've been in and out since.
I'm sober now and think about college.
It is going well and I'm hopeful for the future.
My uncle is still drinking in Kansas
and is happy I'm not there with him.
I struggle to keep clean.
None of it is useless,
everything that has happened
has given me something

Joe

Now that Joe is dead
people are rushing to honor him.
He was a Vietnam veteran.
A sergeant in the Army.
They carried his flag-drapped casket
to the national cemetery
where a cluster of strangers in uniform saluted.
A chaplin prayed, a recording of taps was sounded.
A funeral home donated it's services
to keep him out of the pauper's cemetery.
When Joe was in the hospital
and barely breathing,
doctors hovered over him for a week.
No telling how much money
it cost to keep him alive.
His friends wonder
why attention wasn't given to Joe
as he huddled in the cold,
homeless, psychotic and filthy,
before he was beaten
outside a downtown church
on New Year's eve.
The former soldier was killed
for a few dollars.
We are deeply spiritually ill
if resources for death are so available.
Why aren't resources for life available?
Joe turned up at church,
as so many homeless do.
The pastor let him camp outside the building.
People brought him food
and gave him warm coffee
into his shaking hands
and knew he was growing sicker.

He refused medication.
He refused to move.
The community failed him.
Agencies designed to protect people like Joe
failed him
A long wait for psychiatric beds.
Police refused to arrest Joe.
He was on a public street.
The VA hospital declined
to admit him for treatment.
He was not a threat to himself or others.
Joe was assaulted by thugs
with a paintball gun.
Then beaten to death
all alone in the cold.
Blood stains matted with feathers
were Joe use to sit.
How Joe came to have even a few dollars
is a mystery.
So much about Joe
was a mystery.

Audrey

I celebrated my birthday
in a woman's shelter this year.
20 years ago I was a master sergeant
in the Air Force training enlisted troops.
I'm one face among the thousands
of homeless veterans.
and one of the smaller group of female veterans
who are homeless
and who have endured traumas
that never qualify for a Purple Heart.
I was molested by my grandfather
until I was old enough
to run and climb a tree to get away.
My mom was an alcoholic
and I overcame drug and alcohol abuse.
My first husband committed suicide.
My second marriage was torture
from which I escaped.
Yet today I feel buoyant.
I have undergone a healing of the heart,
digging out the pain.
I had lost my creativity
when the abuse started
I couldn't reach inside myself
and find anything pretty anymore.
I no longer feel I must hide inside
and help others learn skills to recover.
I still want to serve.
My life has been a trial for the road ahead.
I passed a test to have the strength
to pick up and carry more
to accomplish the things in life
I always wanted to do.

Allan

Her son gave his life twice for this country.
His service in Vietnam
and his death by homelessness.
We are all veterans of a domestic war.
It seems like every month they are falling like flies.
Allan was 57 when found dead in the late winter.
Evicted from public housing,
he died of hypothermia.
It was 29 degrees that night.
He spent the weeks between eviction and death
trudging all over the city.
He did not stay in shelters or at Tent City.
He was known for walking.
The body was found in tattered clothes
and his shoes were held together by string.
It took three months to find next of kin
--his mother. Emma is in her eighties
She is in failing health.
Her son in cold storage.
I braced myself for a call
and the return of my son's body
when he was in Vietnam.
I wrote the president
to send my son home before he died.
He lost his mind and his memory in Vietnam.
No one broke through the walls of his silence
and trauma to help him.
The effect of this domestic war
and the targeting, blaming, dehumanization
and isolation is real and the same as any overt war
declared by our government
Death is the inevitable result
and it is neither sweet nor proper.

Harold

I faced the challenges
of finding a home
and tending to my family
on returning from Iraq.
Dozens like me
find themselves
sleeping on the streets,
on friends' couches
or in their cars
within weeks of returning home.
It's horrible
to put your life on the line
and then come back home
to nothing.
I didn't know where to go
or where to turn.
I thought I was alone
but found out
there are a whole lot
of other soldiers
in the same situation.
You can have all of the yellow ribbons
on cars that say Support Our Troops
that you want,
but it's when you take off the uniform
and return to civilian life,
that's when you need support the most.
Asking for help is like saying
I've failed a mission.
It is very hard to do.

Nicole

I’ve got PTSD
but don’t get any benefits yet.
I’m not able to live with my mother
so I found myself walking the streets
of the city with a backpack
full of my belongings
and my one year old daughter
held close.
When I first got back
I just wanted to work
and forget about the war,
but the shock from military
to the real world hit me.
I was depressed for months
and unable to sleep or eat.
The war wasn’t as bad as coming home
because nobody understood
why I was the way I was.
It was a month to month process
trying to function again.
It’s not easy.
It takes time to get on your feet.

Leo

There's a thin line
between despair and hope.
I sleep on a bare mattress
on the carpeted floor
of a warm room for homeless veterans.
Me and three other men share a house.
The walls are almost bare.
On top of the refrigerator
sits an array of pill bottles
which fail to stop the nightmares
I have suffered since returning home
from Vietnam 30 years ago.
I work to stay sober
attending meetings four times a day.
It has been a 36 year battle with the bottle.
A stable place to live
has altered the pattern of crisis.
I have a place that I can call my own
and my feet are grounded.
Hope discovered in the routine of daily life.
I'm proud and wear a Marine cap
but I'm also deeply scarred.
I have wicked, wicked, wicked nightmares.
The VA gives me all kinds of pills to forget.
I say that's not the way to deal with it.
If your willing to sacrifice your life for the country,
I think you should get a little compensation,
especially if you're homeless.

The Numbers

How many veterans are homeless?
How many veterans are there in the US?
No one is sure.
There's no way to tally the number.
There are best estimates
one third of the nation's homeless population
are veterans according to the VA.
200,000 homeless vets
on any given night
on the streets and in shelters.
More veterans are dangerously close
to becoming homeless
or are living in poor conditions.
Nearly half the vets served in Vietnam,
about half the vets on the street suffer
from a mental illness
and three fourths deal with addiction
to alcohol and drugs.
More than 50 percent without a place to live
are Hispanic or African American.
Only 25 percent of the homeless veterans
have service related benefits.

Steve

I walk the streets.
My mission is to help homeless vets
get off the streets.
I'm a 58 year old social worker
who wears wire-rimmed glasses,
my graying hair and mustache
give me a professional look.
I wear a black leather jacket and blue jeans
-- an everyman look for the chilly streets
on the lookout for homeless veterans.
I approach a man who talks fast and moves fast.
The man's gray shoulder-length hair is frizzy,
his eyes a wild look.
He makes large hand gestures
and sounds delusional.
The man is a veteran of the Air Force.
I listen and assess
the man's well being.
After a few minutes,
the man is off,
walking backwards down the street.
I meet another veteran in the shelter.
The building is stuffy and space is tight.
Men, women and a few kids
pack their belongings.
After breakfast, they must leave for the day.
I urge the vet to get some help
but don't force the issue.
My next stops are
the library, the bus depot, under bridges
and in parks looking for veterans who need help.
Vets don't search out help on their own.
They just don't think
they deserve anything

so they don't ask.
People stop asking after a while
and that's the tragedy.
Something pushed these veterans
to the street.
something happened to them
and it scared them.
They know something is wrong
but they are afraid if they ask for help
it is going to be even worse
than it is
because they may lose their freedom.
I was homeless for three years.
There was a period in my life
when I didn't have a place to live.
There was a period in my life
when I needed to go and ask for help.
When you have been homeless
and you have been able to work your way out of it
and create a better life for yourself,
you want others in the same situation
to be part of society working and productive.
You want them to have self esteem and pride.
You want more for them.

Teddy

Hours before his frozen, lifeless body
was found underneath a bridge on Christmas eve,
Larry's homeless friend Teddy
told him he was fed up with life
on the streets.
Teddy was cold.
He was tired.
He was ready to change his life.
But it was to late.
Just after noon Christmas Eve
the middle-aged veteran
was found dead,
wearing just a light jacket
no hat or gloves.
It looked like he fell asleep
and froze to death.
He was frozen solid.
Teddy was not
your typical homeless person
who felt society
owed him something.
He was just on hard times
and didn't know
how to deal with things.
He lived off and on
in a homemade camp
in the woods
near the bridge.
He died
a block
from an emergency cold shelter.

Les

I served in the Navy after high school
and got degrees from Community College
and The University, but back injuries
left me with only a pension
and a struggle to make ends meet.
I'm 59.
I ate a free breakfast at the Armory this morning
and then picked out free clothes.
Volunteers waited to help me
and dozens like me with everything
from medical needs to legal help.
It's called a Stand Down,
a day dedicated to helping those
who served our country
but have fallen on hard times.
It means a lot.
I share a home with five other men.
I'm glad they do this.
Some people are really hurting.
That guy over there
lives in the woods.
They might not have homes
or the finer things in life
but they are still people with dreams.
I dream of self-sufficiency
and after I get a place of my own,
I hope to own a car some day.

Jeff

I enlisted because
it was the only opportunity
for a better life.
I joined the Army after high school.
It was a way to support
a new wife and baby,
It was steady and easy.
I just sent money.
After the service,
I had trouble
finding a good paying job.
I lacked education
and floated
from one minimum wage gig
to the next
cleaning floors, shining shoes
and washing cars.
I have three kids.
I turned to alcohol and drugs.
My wife left.
I ended up on the streets.
Life on the streets
is a vicious cycle.
I turned to crime to survive.
If I could carry it,
I would take it.
If you keep going to the barbershop
you are going to get a haircut.

Joan

My stint in the Army
took me to Europe.
When I got back home
depression left me with nothing
and nowhere to go.
I am 59 and part of a growing population
of women veterans sleeping on the streets.
I cry a lot
when I talk about the events
that left me without a home.
My mother died last year
and I lost everything.
Now I stay in a shelter
and work part-time cleaning phones.
I want to be at a point
where I can help myself.
I'd rather help myself
than be beholden to somebody else.
For years I was unaware
I could get veteran's benefits.
I would be bad off without counseling
I get at the shelter.
I want everybody to know
that the people you see on the streets everyday
..they're not bums.
They are just people with problems
that don't know where to go.
People walk by them
and they give them a sneer and they say
Eww, look at that person...
If everybody would just stop a minute
and ask if they could use some help.
To spend time defending our country
and then to find yourself on the streets
is a tragedy.

Ralph

I was proud to be a Marine.
I felt I did my part.
I can't believe
I'm living like this now.
When I came home,
I had nobody to help me.
I stayed at McDonald's all afternoon
trying to waste time
and found myself riding the bus
the rest of the time.
Veterans are living on the margin,
where housing costs are high,
it can be very tough.
The military recruits from the poor neighborhoods
and makes promises
to teach you job skills and sends you to school.
The reality is a lot of people
come out of the service
and all they know how to do
is be a soldier.
I joined after 9-11
and lost my family when I got home.
I find the normal things
like driving a car difficult.
I swerve around cans in the street
because I fear bombs.
I think it's different than after Vietnam.
People feel they should be helping the soldiers.
I think the only way
I can escape my predicament
is by re-enlisting,
ven if it means
going back to war.

Nadine

I patrolled the train stations after 9-11
as a National Guard member,
then a year in Iraq.
Six months after returning,
I reside in a homeless shelter.
I am just an ordinary person who served.
I am not embarrassed about being homeless.
It's not my fault.
I was unable to cope with life
after daily encounters with insurgent attacks
and bombs.
I had difficulty navigating government red tape
for benefits and simply didn't have enough money
to afford an apartment.
My boyfriend took everything I had
while I was at war
and just vanished.
I live in a shelter
where I share a room
with eight other women.
I'm not angry,
just anxious
to get back on my feet
and find a job.
Even with a college degree in English,
I don't know
when I'll be able to move
out of the shelter.

Clark

I retired when I was 75
from a good paying job.
I'm a combat veteran
of World War II and Korea.
Yet, I am homeless.
I don't consider myself homeless
but I live in a homeless shelter
and the government considers me
a homeless veteran.
Homelessness can happen to anyone.
Most people are a few paychecks away
from knocking on the shelter door.
My path to the shelter
started after my wife died from cancer.
I went belly up.
I lost everything.
It's been downhill since I lost my Hazel.
I packed my bags
and went in search of my brothers and sister.
I found myself sleeping in my car.
It was cold.
I'm bitter towards the government
for abandoning us boys,
the ones who are left.
I don't dwell on my misfortune.
I just chalk it up to a roll of the dice.
I miss a lot of my friends.
I joined the Navy in 1943.
and saw combat in Guam and Okinawa.
I live on $700 a month.
When I entered the shelter,
I was a nervous wreck,
now I don't ever want to leave.
We're like a happy family here.

Randy

I served in South Korea in the 1970's.
I had my share of disturbing experiences.
The war in Iraq
has had a recurrence of my memories.
I think the memories
are the reason I'm jobless
and living in the Veterans Homeless Shelter.
My stress symptoms have increased.
They are provoked by the news of war.
I watch the news and get angry
and shout at the television.
I find myself getting anxious
when I see a veteran in combat
and guns firing on CNN.
I get bad dreams.
It scares me to death.
When I was in Korea,
I was close to war without firing shots
as a person ever will get.
I use to drink away the bad memories.
I was a good ballplayer and student
but when I got out of the service
I was a mess.
I have been in and out of work.
A certain word or noise
triggers my aggression.
I would go off on people.
It wasn't the way
to act in the workplace.
I figured there was something wrong.
I'm not on medication
but counseling
has been an immense help.

Ronny

I was in the Navy
and I couldn't wait to get out.
I can't wait to get back in.
I'm homeless now.
I joined the Navy six years ago.
I was homeless before I enlisted.
I found out after my enlistment was over
that the civilian world was still tough.
When I got out
I thought civilian life would be great.
I thought I hated the Navy,
the officers were always over me
about this and that
but my attitude has changed.
I want to serve for 20 years
and then get out
and be a vet and set.
I was naive and uneducated
about what I could and could not do.
I have been living on the beach
but I don't prefer to think of myself
as homeless.
The world is my home.
It's God's home.
I consider my life in transition,
not homeless.
I appreciate the lessons the Navy taught me
such as discipline and respect for one's self
as well as determination to get things done.
I didn't think I needed an education.
I had all I needed but after living on the streets
with a wife and kid I realized I didn't know anything.
After failing at life again and not having security,
I appreciate the Navy a whole lot more.

Ray

Even booze couldn't chase away the nightmares.
One time a Scud missile landed on the roof of my barracks.
I was in Desert Storm
and I've seen charred bodies, people buried alive,
things you don't forget. The alcohol is self-medicating,
but temporarily. I am 46 and homeless.
I've got PTSD.
I was an Army water purification specialist
during the fighting and since then
I have bounced between shelters,
abandoned warehouses and the streets since 1991.
I just wanted to party and drink.
It finally caught up with me.
When I left for the war, I was all-American
and wanted to be John Wayne.
When I came back,
I was the bitterest person in the world.
You come back off a very intense situation like that
and you look at things differently.
You ask what your role is,
what it is you're meant to do.
I turned to the VA only as a last resort.
I did clean up my act, however in a VA work therapy program.
Now the smell of beer makes me sick.
I hope to be renting my own apartment in a few months.
There's so much negative feeling toward the homeless
but people don't realize what we have gone through.

Robert

People often ask me
what I am going to do with my life.
I tell them
I gave half of my life to my country
and the rest now belongs to me.
I want to be a rebel
and don't want to conform anymore.
I can go to war but when it's all over
I must resume a normal life
and work and live as if there
was never any horror.
It never works that way.
I'm self-conscious
and traumatized by harsh judgment.
I fear everything I touch
is contaminated.
It's hard for me to imagine anything
but negative responses
so I try very little,
becoming distracted
for days, months, years.
A sense of mastery eludes
by a sense of being incompetent.
Invisible like a ghost.
No threat,
just not quite
all here or there.

Dave

I spent two years in the military
and 30 years in pain.
You can't see my wounds.
PTSD has wreaked havoc with my life.
My life has been nothing
but panic attacks, flashbacks and nightmares.
I can't trust nobody.
But, maybe things are going to get better.
I realize I'm not alone.
My pain comes from seeing my best friend
killed in Cambodia.
I feel abandoned.
I came home and went to college
and became a newspaper editor.
After the Gulf war something snapped.
I couldn't handle the homecoming
the troops were getting when it was over.
I was pissed at the world.
I went to the country and became a hermit.
I rarely left the house.
I preferred to remain in surroundings
I could control.
I couldn't work.
I couldn't even take my wife out to dinner.
I didn't even attend my own kids graduations.
I can't say how bad I felt.
I've spent years in therapy
and have only recently started coming out of my shell.
I won't lie.
it's been stressful.
I went shopping with my wife at Costco
and broke out in a sweat.
But I beat the personal demons.
I take things day to day.

Thomas

I was in the Army from 1964 to 1967.
I went to Vietnam
and then struggled with alcoholism.
I live at a home for veterans.
I was lucky to get in.
We got veterans from all the wars
living and waiting to get in here.
Now more younger veterans
are looking for a place to live.
The guys from Iraq and Afghanistan.
The fact they are looking for shelter
pisses me off.
Supporting the troops
is more than a slogan.
Supporting the troops
is putting words into action.
A little outreach to returning veterans now
could save this generation of veterans
from having to live in city shelters.
Most of the residents struggle with problems
like alcoholism. diabetes,
or mental woes like PTSD
I find living here comfortable
because I'm with veterans and we can relate.
These guys are candid
about how much they blame their time in uniform
for what's happened since.
I bottomed out in 1999
when I got divorced and ended up homeless.
I entered rehab and found sobriety.
You know when I came home from the war
you couldn't tell me anything.

Howard

I came home from Vietnam in 1971.
My family told me
to put the war behind me and move on.
I tried. I married and had two kids
and worked in a government job.
But September 11 brought back bad memories.
I started having nightmares and anxiety attacks
and felt angry and guilty.
It took me five or six months to realize
I had a problem.
I needed some help.
My doctor says the war in Iraq
has brought in Vietnam veterans
in increasing numbers seeking help for PTSD.
I have been sensitive to noises ever since Vietnam.
I never did go to a fireworks display.
I did join the National Guard after Vietnam
and found some comfort.
I had a problem relating to people outside the military.
I had lost all my friends because they couldn't relate
to what I went through over in Vietnam.
After 9-11 I felt new fears.
As if I didn't have anyone to back me up.
I felt paranoid in crowds
and my anger sometimes turned to road rage.
This ongoing war is a trigger.
We are really struggling.
We're revisiting our battles.
I feel better these days
as long as I don't watch the news.
I don't want to see the Iraqi vets
go through
what the Vietnam vets went through.
The Iraqi vets need to be treated now –
not 20 years in the future.

Clint

I died
after collapsing in the parking lot
of the VA Medical Center.
The Veteran's hospital staff
called 911 instead of helping me.
My friend had taken me to the hospital
to get treated for asthma and emphysema.
I fought in World War Two and Korea
and now I was dying in front of the VA hospital
and no one inside would help me.
I thought a professional person,
no matter who you are
who has taken an oath to save lives
would help.
They didn't have the right equipment
to help me breath again.
They said calling the fire department
was quicker.
I was 83.
I was a regular patient at the VA for years,
but I was always treated with disrespect
by hospital workers.
My friend said he would never seek care
at the VA Hospital.
He doesn't want to be treated like me.
He gets emotional every time he thinks about it.
They put millions of dollars in a hospital expansion
but cut back on care after 4:30 p.m.
because very few patients came in after hours.
I should have picked a better time
not to die.

Sharon -- Caregiver

I have a simple test
to tell if a veteran
is dealing with PTSD problems.
If a veteran chooses a chair
facing the door,
he probably has it.
If he moves the chair
to block the door
he definitely has it.
They always feel
as if they are always on guard,
in a way
they've never been relieved from duty.
It's all about survival.
I saw PTSD years ago
in my Vietnam veteran boyfriend.
I felt like I wasn't able to help him.
It made me totally confused
but it piqued my interest as a nurse.
I devoted my life
to helping veterans
dealing with the emotional scars of war.
I know why they hurt.
When you know absolutely
without a doubt that you're gonna die
and then you don't die,
at that moment you lost your personal sense of safety.
What is more emotional than almost dying?
I tell them that just talking about the feelings
will help and that it will get better.
Once they cry
they truly are feeling
and that nothing could ever be harder
than what they've already been through.

Lynn

I think I have every right to curse,
but it's something I'm not likely to do.
I have to shout at some administrative type.
Here take my credit card
if it means I can get my boy home.
The VA said they would pay to transfer
my son home.
Is he being treated differently
because he wasn't hurt in Iraq?
Ben can't speak, move or even scratch his nose.
I'm the kind of woman
the government has appealed to
during the past five years
about the nobility of military service.
I've already sent two sons to Iraq.
Ben was on leave when he got injured
in a dirt bike accident.
It was a massive brain injury.
After surgery he could feed himself
and get around with a walker.
Then one morning
he fell on his way to the bathroom
and hit his head.
I begged the staff to examine my son
but no one did.
Ben started vomiting and went limp.
So there were more surgeries.
My son cannot sit up now.
He cannot talk or otherwise communicate with me.
I want my boy out of the VA.
I used Ben's military insurance
to move him to Colorado for treatment.
That was $14,000.
He is doing well and healing properly
at the private rehab center.

Caroline

My husband John
fought for his nation in World War II.
Then he came home
and fought for himself.
John was 84 when he died in 2004.
They took my man,
chewed him up, spit him out
and give him back to me.
The VA never regarded him as being ill.
You had to have a scar.
His nerves were his scar.
Changed by war.
We were married in 1941.
Nine months later
John was called into the Army.
Two years later he was discharged
after being hurt in an explosion in Italy.
It took him another two years to recover.
He was not the same man
when he came home
and for years
I had to walk a mental minefield with him
because of his war experiences.
When he would get nervous or in trouble
he would become insane.
He could not shake the image of a dead buddy.
Once he shred my woolen housecoat
that he had bought for me
while I was still wearing it.
I hid the silverware
so he wouldn't hurt himself
or someone else.
John worked as a trucker
and built his own home.
The VA said John's condition
was a matter of opinion.

The families of veterans
should be prepared by
the government for the
return of their loved ones.
I've always been puzzled
at the treatment veterans get.
I'm not saying they should
come back and get carte blanche
but the hoops they have to jump
through to get any benefits
at all are ridiculous.

Joseph

I’m ready to put down roots.
It’s the first time in decades.
I was in Korea and Vietnam
and am 71 years old.
I have been roaming North
and South America and I
am tired of moving.
I got hooked on drugs
in Vietnam. I quit cold turkey.
Drugs turn you into an idiot.
It’s nearly impossible to save
enough money to put down
on an apartment.
I am trying to get into a group home.

John

My friends are coming to terms
a day after I killed myself outside
the VA Hospital.
They wonder why I shot myself
with a handgun. I left a note
and said I was protesting the war.
I had the demons of Vietnam.
It was time to go.
I had to make a statement about
the growing number young
veterans getting injured
and the medical treatment
offered by the VA.
The VA was screwing people
bad. I hated see seeing
young people getting
killed and getting inadequate
treatment.
I had cancer and PTSD
and did what I had to do.
People say I had a big heart
for a big man and that I
was bigger than life…
a big teddy bear.
But I was tortured
by memories.

It's been three years since
I left Baghdad.
Now I am trying to make
it through the VA system.
I'm barely getting by,
flirting with homelessness
and turned down for a dozen
jobs. I am trying to get
treatment for PTSD.
Too many veterans share
my difficulties in readjusting
to life in America.
When you join the Army
they tell you they have
your back until the end.
From my experience, it
hasn't been that way.
When this war started
there was a level and
anticipation and planning
that was insufficient.
Veterans are overwhelming
the system.
I am still haunted by
what I saw in Iraq.
I have all the tell-tale
signs of PTSD.
I am seeing a VA
counselor. but have
been denied compensation.
I am living off the education
benefits with my parents.
My future is uncertain.
Things are getting worse
and worse. I do what I can.
It's not enough.

Mike

The images on TV of Americans
fighting and dying in Iraq
are traumatizing Vietnam vets
all over again. Even though I
am a patriotic guy, I am angry
we are even in Iraq.
I'm having trouble talking
with my wife. I have been
married three times.
I can't stand the government
or authority figures.
I'm not going to let anyone
tell me what to do. That
makes keeping a job difficult.
I must have had 20 jobs.
You know some Vietnam vets
still haven't sought help after
all these years. A lot of guys
think their treatment will be
terminated because the returning
War on Terror vets are going to
overwhelm the system.

Will

My father
wondered if there was anything
he could do to help me.
It was a big shock
when I had entered the Army.
The family didn't expect me to enlist.
When I wrote home from basic training
all I was told to do was kill, kill, kill, kill...
When I came home from the war
I seemed in pretty good shape
but stayed at home and drank.
My father had done the same thing
after World War II.
My father minimized his four years
in the South Pacific with the Marines
and tried more or less to forget about it.
He didn't have any nightmares
but certain dates were bad...
like Christmas.
When my father was a kid on the farm
he never thought of war
and was totally unprepared.
We used to get together
but the I haven't been back home
since my mother's died in 1985.

Brendan

Hell is group therapy.
The talk is mostly bullshit.
There are a lot of war stories.
How true they are is anyone's guess.
I sit silent in the corner.
I think we are in group for our war crimes
by appointment of the devil.
Tell the doctors what you are feeling.
What is the problem?
Why are you angry.?
I'm fed up with being a veteran.
Group therapy is driving me nuts.
Don't they understand?
I have gone to war.
I hurt.
Don't tell me how to act
or what to do.
Therapy is Mickey Mouse crap.
I don't want to make any damn wallet.
I have no money to put in it.
I don't want to paint a picture of the Last Supper
Jesus doesn't give a damn about me, either.
Let me create what I want,
not what the system wants.
Let me dream.

Dutch

It's Hell's House.
The Vet's Home is a place
for old, sick, and homeless veterans.
The buildings are from another century,
worn like the men and women they house.
How did I get into this mess?
I just wanted to be a normal person
and live a happy life.
What will happen to me?
Will I ever leave the Home
on my own power
or on a morgue cart?
It's like being in film noir.
My room is dark, hot, and colorless.
The stench of urine rises from the carpet
I sit by the window eating
and watching as men shuffle back and forth
between the buildings.
The buildings condemned
just like the residents.
Men worry about what will become of them.

Home Without A Home

I travel with a heavy backpack
strapped across my shoulders,
and a plastic bag of clothes.
When you are homeless,
these are the things you carry.
And tucked away somewhere
are the memories of a war
that are still fresh.
No yellow ribbons greeted me
when I returned home.
Now I soldier on each day
trying to find some place to call my own,
riding late night buses to shelters
only to be rousted out at dawn.
A private first class,
now a second class war veteran
walking the dark streets.
Home but without a home.

www.ingramcontent.com/pod-product-compliance
Ingram Content Group UK Ltd.
Pitfield, Milton Keynes, MK11 3LW, UK
UKHW041838200726
13854UKWH00003BA/1198

9 781435 731301